PIGGLES' GUIDE TO...

AEROPLANES

BY KIRSTY HOLMES

BookLife
PUBLISHING

©2018
BookLife Publishing
King's Lynn
Norfolk PE30 4LS

All rights reserved.
Printed in Malaysia.

A catalogue record for this
book is available from the
British Library.

ISBN: 978-1-78637-494-3

Written by:
Kirsty Holmes

Edited by:
Holly Duhig

Designed by:
Danielle Rippengill

IMAGE CREDITS

CONTENTS

WORDS THAT LOOK LIKE <u>this</u> CAN BE FOUND IN THE GLOSSARY ON PAGE 24.

WELCOME TO FLIGHT SCHOOL!

So you're interested in aeroplanes? Do you dream of soaring through the skies, or climbing through the clouds? Then you've come to the right place! The Sty in the Sky Flight School!

STY IN THE SKY
ACADEMY
EARN YOUR WINGS

Here, you will learn all you need to know about some amazing flying machines, and join the **elite** flying force known as the Pink Wings! So pay attention: it's time to FLY!

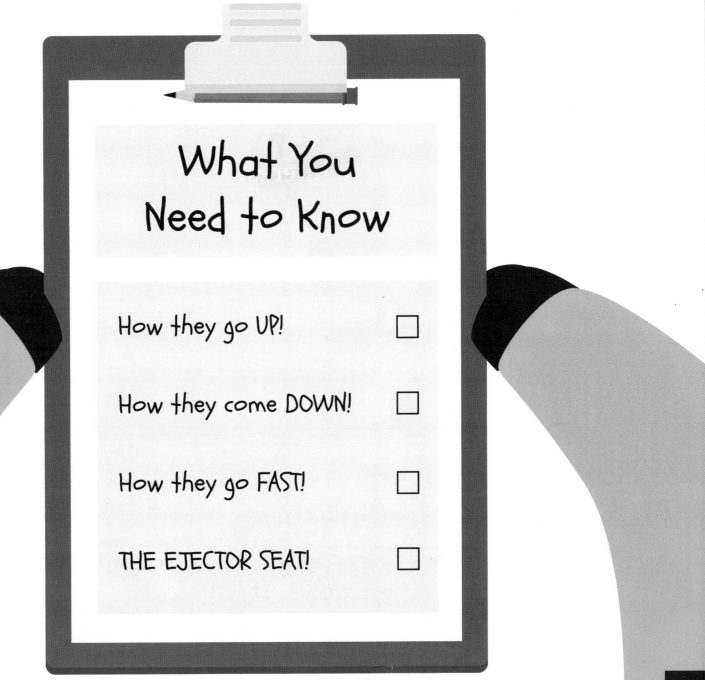

What You Need to Know

How they go UP! ☐

How they come DOWN! ☐

How they go FAST! ☐

THE EJECTOR SEAT! ☐

LESSON 1:
WHAT IS AN AEROPLANE?

MILITARY JET

STUNT PLANE

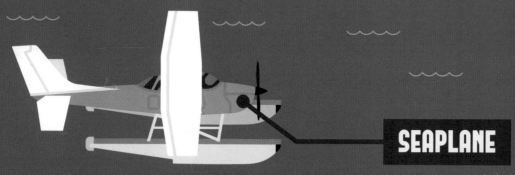

SEAPLANE

Aeroplanes are a type of aircraft – this means a flying machine! They can be used to transport passengers or **cargo**.

They can be small enough for just one person, or big enough to carry hundreds of people all over the world!

PASSENGER PLANE

CARGO PLANE

PAPER PLANE

Now then class; who threw this? Stop messing about!

7

PARTS OF AN AEROPLANE

FIXED WINGS

Aeroplane wings are fixed in place. They create lift and keep the aeroplane in the sky.

Let's look at the parts of an aeroplane.

FUSELAGE

This is the main body. It holds everything together and carries the passengers or cargo.

AEROPLANES ARE ALL DIFFERENT, BUT WILL HAVE THESE SAME BASIC PARTS.

POWERED

All aeroplanes are powered. They either have a jet engine or a propeller. (Learn more about power in Lesson 5!).

COCKPIT

This is where the pilot sits to control the aeroplane.

NOSE

Most aeroplanes will have a nose shaped like a cone.

LESSON 3:
INSIDE AN AEROPLANE

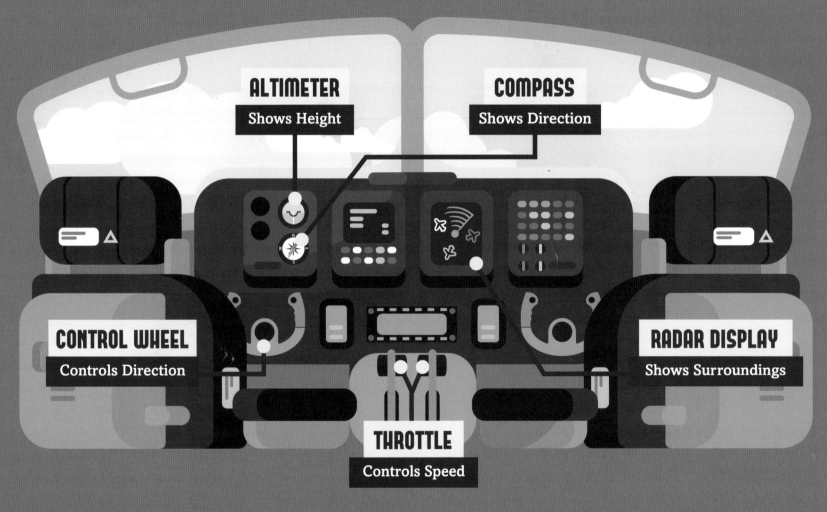

ALTIMETER
Shows Height

COMPASS
Shows Direction

CONTROL WHEEL
Controls Direction

RADAR DISPLAY
Shows Surroundings

THROTTLE
Controls Speed

The pilot sits in the cockpit. It has all the controls a pilot needs to fly. The <u>instruments</u> give the pilot important information about the plane and the weather.

The middle of the aeroplane contains the cabin.

LUGGAGE, CARGO AND EVEN ANIMALS ARE STORED IN THE TAIL OR BELLY OF THE PLANE, CALLED THE HOLD.

CABIN CREW

Passengers sit here. Cabin crew look after the passengers during flights and show them how to stay safe and comfortable.

LESSON 4: LIFT!

To get an aeroplane into the sky, you need to create lift. Lift is a **force** which pushes the aeroplane upwards. Four main forces act on an aeroplane when it is flying:

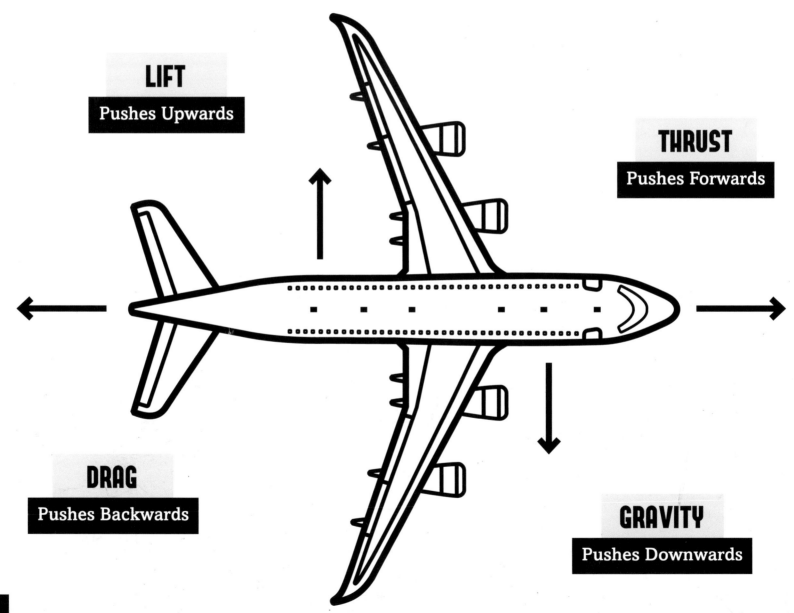

LIFT
Pushes Upwards

THRUST
Pushes Forwards

DRAG
Pushes Backwards

GRAVITY
Pushes Downwards

The aeroplane's wings create lift. They have a special shape, which makes air move faster over the curved top of the wing.

LOW PRESSURE

LIFT

HIGH PRESSURE

The air below the wing has more **pressure**, while the air above has less pressure. This lifts the wings into the air.

THRUST!

To create lift, the plane needs to be moving.
To move forward, we need to create thrust.

PROPELLER

PROPELLERS

Propellers are like big fans. They spin and, just like the wings,
change the air pressure and pull the aeroplane forwards.
Propellers usually need an engine to make them spin.

JET ENGINES

Jet engines work by taking in a lot of air very quickly, then pushing it out of the back of the engine as a high-speed jet of gas.

JET ENGINES ARE VERY LOUD! CAN YOU ALL HEAR ME?

The force of this air being sucked in and spat out of the engine pushes the aeroplane forwards and creates thrust.

LESSON 6:
TAKEOFF AND LANDING

Getting into the air is called 'takeoff'. Most aeroplanes take off from a **runway**. The aeroplane will drive along the runway, getting faster and faster. The pilot uses the controls to increase the lift on the wings, and the aeroplane lifts into the air.

At the end of a flight, the aeroplane lands. The first part of landing is called descent. The pilot slowly flies lower and lower towards the runway, and slows down. The pilot puts down the landing gear, and the plane rolls to a stop.

Some planes land on water, on large ships, or even on snow using giant skis!

LESSON 7:
FAMOUS PLANES

AMELIA EARHART

Amelia Earhart became the first female <u>aviator</u> to fly solo across the Atlantic Ocean in 1928.

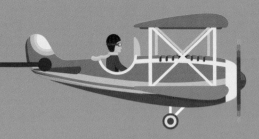

SPIRIT OF ST. LOUIS

The Spirit of St. Louis became the first plane to cross the Atlantic Ocean without stopping in 1927.

AIR FORCE ONE

The president of the USA has their own special jet aeroplane, called Air Force One.

FIRST EVER POWERED AEROPLANE FLIGHT

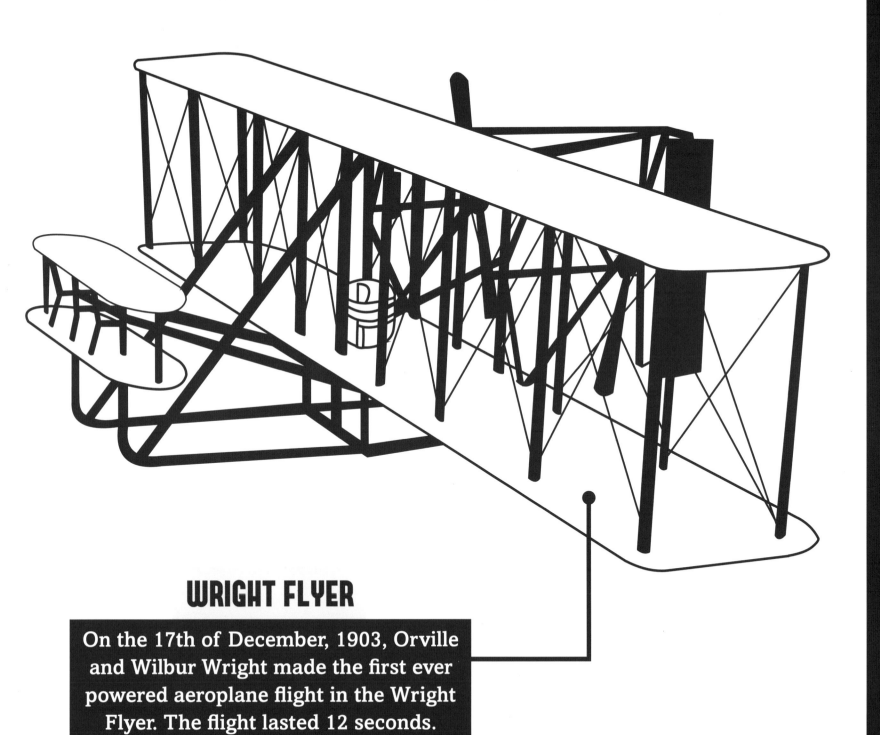

WRIGHT FLYER

On the 17th of December, 1903, Orville and Wilbur Wright made the first ever powered aeroplane flight in the Wright Flyer. The flight lasted 12 seconds.

FLIGHT CHECK

OK, students – let's test your knowledge about aeroplanes and see if you've been paying attention! Get them all right, and you earn your Pink Wings!

Questions

1. What is the name of the force that pushes an aeroplane upwards?

2. Where does the pilot sit?

3. List three types of aeroplane from pages 6 and 7.

4. Name one way an aeroplane creates thrust.

5. Which instrument controls speed?

Did you get all the answers right? You did? Well done!

This means you are now an expert aviator and you have become a member of the world's most elite flying force: The Pink Wings!

BONUS LESSON:
EJECTOR SEAT!

Pilots have to learn all about aeroplanes and spend many years learning to fly them safely. They have to know how to take off and land the aeroplane, and what to do in an emergency...

STEP ONE
Identify Emergency

"WE'VE RUN OUT OF PEANUTS!"

STEP TWO
Don't Panic

STEP THREE
Grab Parachute

GLOSSARY

AVIATOR   someone who flies an aircraft

CARGO   goods carried by a vehicle

ELITE   someone or something which is the best of a group

FORCE   a power or energy

INSTRUMENTS   a tool or device for doing a job

PRESSURE   a steady force acting on a surface

RUNWAY   a smooth, level strip where aeroplanes land

INDEX